MASTERING LIFE
with the
TWELVE STEPS
for
CHRISTIAN LIVING

By Ron Keller

A daily Scriptural guide
and journal for
Steps One through Four

This manuscript contains no direct quotations from any Bible. I wish to acknowledge that most passages were based on texts from the Jerusalem Bible (Doubleday & Company, Garden City, New York) and Today's English Version Good News for Modern Man (American Bible Society, New York, New York). Most Scriptural passages have been paraphrased, adapted or rewritten primarily to make the language more inclusive. Each section includes Scriptural references for the student who is interested in more literal translation or in-depth study.

I wish to express my appreciation to Donald A. Keller for his conception of the logo.

Mastering Life with the Twelve Steps of Christian Living

Copyright © 1989 Prince of Peace Publishing, Inc.

All rights reserved. No portion of this book may be reproduced in any form, except for brief quotations in reviews, without the written permission of the publishers.

Library of Congress Catalog Card Number

Keller, J. Ronald, 1945

Bibliography: p.

ISBN 0-933173-172

Printed in the United States of America

Ron Keller, program director for the Institute for Christian Living, has done extensive work with the twelve-step process through Ala-Teen, Adult Children of Alcoholics, Al-Anon, small groups, and Twelve Steps for Christian Living groups. As program director for ICL, he has developed and is implementing a training program for group leaders.

He was an area/regional director of Young Life for 13 years. He served on the N.D. State Pardon Board for eleven years, and on the Heartview Alcoholism Treatment Center Board for seven years. Mr. Keller is the former chair of the department of Youth Ministry at Barrington College in Barrington, Rhode Island. He has been a consultant/trainer for Youth Forum, Youth Leadership, Tentmakers, the Catholic Church, Renew, and the ICL. He is an adjunct professor at Luther/Northwestern and Bethel Seminaries in Minneapolis and St. Paul and has an M.A. in Theology from Fuller Seminary. He is also a sailor and a writer.

Institute for Christian Living
855 Pennsylvania Avenue North
Golden Valley, Minnesota 55427
(612) 593-1791

The Institute for Christian Living is a service of Riverside Medical Center, a joint venture of St. Mary's and Fairview Riverside hospitals.

Prepared for those who seek personal and spiritual growth

For many years, I have used and shared the concepts in this book in a number of ways. The encouragement they have given to me and to numerous others has consistently prodded me to get it into print. As you read and participate in the exercises, it is my hope that you too will see yourself more clearly, get a better sense of what you really want to accomplish, and receive encouragement to take the risks needed to move ahead toward the fulfillment of your dreams.

I have experienced and heard others express a need for a way to break into a richer, more spiritual lifestyle. <u>Mastering Life with the Twelve Steps of Christian Living</u> is hopefully one of the tools that responds to that need. Most people feel inadequate or unworthy of exploring the spiritual dimension of life. To some people, this seems scary or overwhelming. I have tried to address these fears and concerns. This book is a series of short, concise readings, integrating scriptural paraphrases with The Twelve Steps for Christian Living. This integration has enabled a simple, gentle and understandable approach to personal and spiritual growth.

<u>Mastering Life with the Twelve Steps of Christian Living</u> is a 70-day guide which invites the reader to spend twelve minutes each day reading and reflecting on the passages. In applying these words to my own life, most of my personal growth has taken place through consistency, repetition, and application of what I have learned. These readings have become an actual part of me, as word by word I have let them soak into my heart and mind, nourishing and encouraging me toward a richer, more fruitful life.

Dedicated to all the mentors in my life,
especially my family of origin;
Nancy, my mentor in joy;
and my children, Brigitte Anne, Joshua John and
Jonathan Paul.

Contents

How to use this book 9
The Twelve Steps for Christian Living 12

Step One 15

    The act of surrender 16
    Embracing the passage of time 20
    Evaluating your habits 24
    Accepting yourself as you are 28
    Managing your life 32
    Having your life filled with God's presence 38
    Evaluation chart 44

Step Two 45

    Striving for a balanced perspective 46
    Receiving and giving love 52
    The importance of daily prayer
        and meditation 58
    Expressing gratitude 66
    Finding wholeness in the person of
        Jesus Christ 72
    Extending yourself to another 82
    Seeing yourself as a student 86
    Seeing yourself as a teacher 90
    The willingness to pay the price 94
    Evaluation chart 100

Step Three 101

    The importance of taking care of yourself 102
    The importance of relationships 106
    The importance of being involved with
        others who can give support 114
    The importance of extending yourself 122
    Evaluation chart 126

Step Four 127

    You need something to live for, a vision
        that is your own 128
    Appreciating your own uniqueness 134
    Pressing for the full use of your potential 138
    Seeking out and exercising your gifts
        and talents 142
    Being positive 148
    Having clear, attainable, measurable
        goals 152
    Learning to be persistent 156
    Responding to the vision I am given 162
    The standard of excellence 166
    Evaluation chart 170

Afterword 171
Presentations and Workshops 173

HOW TO USE THIS BOOK...

In order to get the most out of this book, the reader needs to spend at least 12 minutes each day on the designated step and exercises. Six minutes in the morning and six minutes at night are ideal.

Each section of the book contains the following:

1. *One of the twelve steps.*

2. *An important passage to read each day.* Memorize it. Read it out loud. Talk about it to others. Do not rush through the reading. Read only the designated passage for the day, even if it seems brief.

3. *A page for your personal reflections.* At the end of each day, indicate on this page:

   - how many times you read the passage;
   - the degree to which you applied the passage to your life today. (Rate yourself on a scale from one to ten, ten being the highest.)

4. *One or two blank pages* for your personal journal entries. Write, draw, or scribble on these pages. Use them as a diary or make entries about the designated passage and the influence it is having on your life.

5. *An evaluation chart* at the end of each section (pages 44, 100, 126, and 170). Chart your growth and progress day by day. Indicate your rating for the day by placing a dot on the chart provided. When you have

completed that section, connect the dots. When you finish the book, review the four charts to discover the cycles, seasons and patterns in your life.

Learn to act on what you read. Do what you sense the passage is telling you to do.

Dr. Vernon J. Bittner is a living demonstration of how important and effective the Twelve Steps for Christian living can be. From the depths of despair and attempted suicide, he reached out to apply the Twelve Steps to his own life. He creatively adapted the Twelve Steps of Alcoholics Anonymous to his own life situation and wrote the <u>Twelve Steps for Christian Living</u>.

For more than thirty years he has tried and tested the principles of these Twelve Steps. He, like others, has discovered a crucial and adventurous lifestyle, a gentle yet motivating approach to life. In 1980, Dr. Bittner and a group of others founded the Institute for Christian Living (ICL). As the executive director of the ICL, Dr. Bittner continues in his life-long commitment to bring health and wholeness to all. He has written five books that nurture spiritual and group growth through the twelve-step process. <u>You Can Help With Your Healing</u> has a broad circulation throughout the United States.

Twelve Steps for Christian Living

by Dr. Vernon J. Bittner
1987©, Prince of Peace Publishing Co.

1. We admit our need for God's gift of salvation, that we are powerless over certain areas of our lives and that our lives are at times sinful and unmanageable.

2. We come to believe through the Holy Spirit that a power who came in the person of Jesus Christ and who is greater than ourselves can transform our weaknesses into strengths.

3. We make a decision to turn our wills and our lives over to the care of Jesus Christ as we understand Him, hoping to understand Him more fully.

4. We make a searching and fearless moral inventory of ourselves, both our strengths and our weaknesses.

5. We admit to Christ, to ourselves, and to another human being the exact nature of our sins.

6. We become entirely ready to have Christ heal all of these defects of character that prevent us from having a more spiritual lifestyle.

7. We humbly ask Christ to transform all of our shortcomings.

8. We make a list of all persons we have harmed and become willing to make amends to them all.

9. We make direct amends to such persons wherever possible, except when to do so would injure them or others.

10. We continue to take personal inventory and when we are wrong, promptly admit it, and when we are right, thank God for the guidance.

11. We seek through prayer and meditation to improve our conscious contact with Jesus Christ, as we understand Him, praying for knowledge of God's will for us and the power to carry that out.

12. Having experienced a new sense of spirituality as a result of these steps and realizing that this is a gift of God's grace, we are willing to share the message of Christ's love and forgiveness with others and to practice these principles for spiritual living in all our affairs.

Revised 10/20/87

STEP ONE

We admit our need for God's gift of salvation, that we are powerless over certain areas of our lives, and that our lives are at times sinful and unmanageable.

For most people, the first step is the most difficult. It is the step that they keep going back to. The readings for the next 14 days will help in the continuous struggle to admit the way things really are, acknowledge powerlessness, and recognize that our lives are at times unmanageable.

Days 1 and 2	The act of surrender
Days 3 and 4	Embracing the passage of time
Days 5 and 6	Evaluating your habits
Days 7 and 8	Accepting yourself as you are
Days 9-11	Managing your life
Days 12-14	Having your life filled with God's presence

Step One reminds us of our need to surrender, to trust, to Let Go and Let God.

Reading for days 1 and 2

(To the reader: Read this passage several times during the day. Don't rush through it. Think about it, and maybe even talk about it to others.)

I, Jesus, am telling you not to worry about your life and what you are to eat, nor about your body and what kind of clothes you are to wear. Surely life means more than food, and the body more than clothing! Look at the birds in the sky. They don't sow or reap or gather into barns; yet the Lord feeds them. Are you not worth much more than they are? *Can any of you, for all your worrying, add one single minute to your life span?* And why worry about clothing? Think of the flowers growing in the fields; they never have to work or spin; yet I assure you that not even Solomon in all his regalia was robed like one of these. Now if that is how God clothes the grass in the field which is there today and thrown into the furnace tomorrow, will the Lord not much more look after you, you of little faith? So do not worry; do not say, "What are we to eat? What are we to drink? How are we to be clothed?" It is the pagans who set their hearts on all these things. Your heavenly Master knows you need them all. *Set your hearts first, on the Lord's kingdom* and righteousness, and all these other things will be given you as well. So, don't worry about tomorrow: tomorrow will take care of itself. Each day has enough trouble of its own.

Based on Matthew 6: 25-34 (JB)

(To the reader: This format will continue for 70 days. Be sure to reflect on the reading and record your reflections each day.)

PERSONAL REFLECTIONS

The act of surrender

Day 1 (Be sure to make daily entries on the chart on page 44.)

Number of times the passage was read: 3

Today, I trusted. I was not anxious. I did not worry. I realized that worrying adds nothing to my life.

Degree to which I applied the passage to my life today (10 highest, 1 lowest): 8

Day 2

Number of times the passage was read: 2

Today I lived as if it was the last 24 hours of my life. I surrendered, relaxed, and enjoyed life.

Degree to which I applied the passage to my life today: 3

It's not easy to relate to the passages on page 17, when 3 small children are dependent on your ability to provide for their needs.
On the other hand, too much focus is often directed to the accumulation of material possessions; our time spent on our careers tells the true story.

Step One is a reminder that we are more content when we gracefully embrace the passage of time.

Reading for days 3 and 4

There is a season for everything,
a time for every season under heaven:

> a time for giving birth,
> a time for dying;
> a time for planting,
> a time for uprooting what has been planted.
> a time for killing,
> a time for healing;
> a time for knocking down,
> a time for building up.
> a time for tears,
> a time for mourning,
> a time for dancing.
> a time for throwing stones away,
> a time for gathering them up;
> a time for embracing,
> a time to refrain from embracing.
> a time for searching,
> a time for losing;
> a time for keeping,
> a time for throwing away.
> a time for tearing,
> a time for sewing;
> a time for keeping silent,
> a time for speaking.
> a time for loving,
> a time for hating;
> a time for war,
> a time for peace.

Even in laughter the heart finds sadness, and joy makes way for sorrow.

Based on Ecclesiastes 3: 1-8 and Proverbs 14:13 (JB)

PERSONAL REFLECTIONS

Embracing the passage of time

Day 3

Number of times the passage was read: _____

Today, I accepted the flow of life, the passage of time, the seasons and cycles. I recognized that there is an appropriate time for everything.

Degree to which I applied the passage to my life today: _____

Day 4

Number of times the passage was read: _____

Today, more than ever, I acknowledged God as the Master of time and the Lord of life. I gave thanks for my birth. At the same time, I embraced my coming death.

Degree to which I applied the passage to my life today: _____

We admit that our lives are at times sinful and unmanageable.

Step One reminds us to evaluate and surrender our habits.

Reading for days 5 and 6

It is God who puts both the will and the action into you.

There is nothing I cannot master with the help of Jesus, the one who gives me strength.

All I can say is that I forget the past and *I press on* toward what is still to come.

The person who looks steadily at the perfect law of freedom and makes that the habit---not listening and then forgetting, but actively putting it into practice---will be happy in all things.

You have stripped off your old behavior with your old self, and you have put on a new self which will continually be renewed in the image of your Creator.

Based on Phillipians 2:13; 4:13; 3:13b; James 1:22-25; Colossians 3:7-10 (JB)

PERSONAL REFLECTIONS

Evaluating your habits

Day 5

Number of times the passage was read: _____

Today, I acknowledged that God is at work in my life. I will be given both the desire and the ability to do what God wants me to do.

Degree to which I applied the passage to my life today: _____

Day 6

Number of times the passage was read: _____

Today, I trusted Jesus Christ. I am convinced that in faith I can do all things. I believe old habits can be conquered and new ones developed.

Degree to which I applied the passage to my life today: _____

Accepting life, the passage of time, and the unmanageable parts of our lives, and *accepting ourselves* just as we are...... this is the message of Step One and the pathway to peace and serenity.

Reading for days 7 and 8

My brothers and sisters, because of God's great mercy to us I appeal to you: *Offer ourselves as a living sacrifice to God.* This is the true worship that you should offer.

For it is not as if we had a *high priest, Jesus Christ, who was incapable of feeling our weaknesses with us;* but we have one who has been tempted in every way that we are, though he is without sin. Let us be confident then, in approaching the throne of grace through him, that we shall have mercy from him and find grace when we are in need of help.

Those who are in Christ Jesus are not condemned. The law of the spirit of life in Christ Jesus has set you free from the law of sin and death.

Based on Romans 12:1; Hebrews 4:15-16; Romans 8:1 (TEV and JB)

PERSONAL REFLECTIONS

Accepting yourself as you are

Day 7

Number of times the passage was read: _____

Today, I take comfort in the truth that Jesus Christ came as a human being and is capable of empathizing with me, my feelings and experiences. I accepted his ability to carry me through or deliver me from discouraging human experiences.

Degree to which I applied the passage to my life today: _____

Day 8

Number of times the passage was read: _____

Today, I will accept myself as I am.

Degree to which I applied the passage to my life today: _____

Many parts of our lives seem unmanageable. We may feel powerless about these areas. It is these feelings that remind us of our need to surrender the management of our lives to God as revealed in the person of Jesus Christ.

Reading for days 9, 10, and 11

Jesus says, *Come to me,* all of you who are tired from carrying heavy loads, and *I will give you rest.* Take my yoke and put it on you, and learn from me, because I am gentle and humble in spirit; and you will find rest. For the yoke I will give you is easy, and the load I will put on you is not heavy.

Jesus says, Listen, *I stand at the door* and knock; if anyone hears my voice and opens the door, I will come into your house and eat with you and you will eat with me.

The Lord is my shepherd.
I shall not want. You make me lie down in green pastures. *You lead me* to still waters. You restore my soul and lead me in the paths of righteousness. Even though I walk through the valley of the shadow of death, I will fear no evil, for you, Lord are *with me.* Your rod and your staff, they comfort me. In the presence of my enemies, you prepare a feast before me. You anoint my head with oil. My cup runs over. Surely goodness and mercy will follow me all the days of my life. And afterwards, I will dwell in your house forever and ever.

God's plan is to make known a secret, a rich and glorious secret for all peoples. And the secret is simply this: *Christ is in you,* which means that you will share in the glory of God.

(Reading continued on next page)

Trust in the Lord with all your heart. Never rely on what you think you know. Remember the Lord in everything you do, and you will be shown the right way. Never let yourself think that you are wiser than you are; simply obey the Lord and refuse to do wrong.

Based on Matthew 11:28-30; Revelation 3:20; Psalm 23:1-6; Colossians 1:27; Proverbs 3: 5-7; (TEV and JB)

PERSONAL REFLECTIONS

Managing your life

Day 9

Number of times the passage was read: _____

Today, I came to Jesus Christ. I accepted his "yoke" for me. In doing this, I expressed my desire to have him manage my life.

Degree to which I applied the passage to my life today: _____

Day 10

Number of times the passage was read: _____

Today, I listened to his knock upon my door. I realized that only I can open the door. I let him in.

Degree to which I applied the passage to my life today: _____

Day 11

Number of times the passage was read: _____

Today, I acknowledged that Jesus Christ is my leader, shepherd and manager. Under the Lord's care, I have everything that I need. I surrendered the management of my life to Jesus today.

Degree to which I applied the passage to my life today: _____

.... and when we surrender our hearts, minds, and wills to Jesus Christ, then the Holy Spirit, Counselor, Comforter, Advocate, Helper and Bearer of gifts and fruits comes to reside within the surrendered one...

to heal,
encourage,
empower and
equip for life.

Reading for days 12, 13, and 14

God gives the Holy Spirit to those who ask.

You will receive power when the Holy Spirit comes on you.

Jesus says, I shall ask God and *you will be given another Advocate to be with you forever.*

I have said these things to you while still with you; but the Advocate, the Holy Spirit, whom God will send in my name, will teach you everything and remind you of all I have said to you.

Still, I must tell you the truth: it is for your own good that I am going, because unless I go, the Advocate will not come to you.

I still have many things to say to you, but they would be too much for you now. But when the Spirit of Truth comes, you will be led to complete truth; and you will be told of the things to come. The Spirit of Truth will glorify me.

Here is what the Spirit brings: fruits of love, joy, peace, patience, kindness, goodness, trustfulness, gentleness and self-control.

Based on Luke 11:13; Acts 1:8a; John 14:16,25; 16:7-15; Galatians 5:22 (JB and TEV)

PERSONAL REFLECTIONS

Having your life filled with God's presence

<u>Day 12</u>

Number of times the passage was read: _____

Today, I asked the Holy Spirit to come into my life more fully. I recognized that the Spirit is a powerful person working in, through, and around me.

Degree to which I applied the passage to my life today: _____

<u>Day 13</u>

Number of times the passage was read: _____

Today, I was thankful that I have been given another "advocate" to be with me forever. This "comforter" will teach me and lead me into complete truth.

Degree to which I applied the passage to my life today: _____

<u>Day 14</u>

Number of times the passage was read: _____

Today, I opened myself to receive the fruits of the Holy Spirit. These abiding fruits will be reminders of the continuous presence and guidance of the Holy Spirit.

Degree to which I applied the passage to my life today: _____

Lord Jesus, I want to surrender my life. This is gradually becoming my heart's desire. I have come to understand that surrender is the cornerstone for growth. It is the platform on which all else in my life is built.

I realize now, like never before, that I must surrender. As hard as it will be, I intend to forfeit my rights. I want to surrender my habits. I want to give You my plans and the use of my time.

Honestly, I must admit that I am afraid. Please give me the courage to surrender. Give me the ability to give myself to you just as I am. I want to be willing to come stripped of all my personal desires, except one... the desire to serve you.

To you, Lord, I give my life... my feelings, schedule, resources, work load, gifts and ideas. To you, I give myself.

I understand that I am surrendering to you, a living God, a personal God. In surrendering to you, I am bound to find my freedom.

Lord Jesus, I want to do all this and more. I want to learn to love you.

Let your words become mine...

And going on a little further, Jesus fell on his face and prayed, "Lord, if it is possible, let this cup pass me by. Let it be as you, not I would, have it."

Then to all gathered he said, "If you want to be a follower of mine, renounce yourself, take up your cross every day and follow me. For if you want to save your life, you will lose it; but if you lose your life for my sake, you will save it. What gain is it for you to have won the world and to have lost or ruined your very self."

Come near to God, and God will come near to you.

Based on Matthew 26:39; Luke 9: 23-25; James 4:8 (TEV & JB)

EVALUATION CHART

How surrendered is my life becoming?

+   Today I surrendered my life and did not try to control it.
0   Today I wanted to control my life.
-   Today I controlled by life and did not consider surrendering it.

								Day						
1	2	3	4	5	6	7	8	9	10	11	12	13	14	
														10
								+						9
														8
														7
														6
								0						5
														4
														3
								-						2
														1

STEP TWO

We come to believe through the Holy Spirit that a power who came in the person of Jesus Christ and who is greater than ourselves can transform our weaknesses into strengths.

Days 15-18	Striving for a balanced perspective
Days 19-21	Receiving and giving love
Days 22-24	The importance of daily prayer and meditation
Days 25-26	Expressing gratitude
Days 27-31	Finding wholeness in the person of Jesus Christ
Days 32-33	Extending yourself to another
Days 34-35	Seeing yourself as a student
Day 36	Seeing yourself as the teacher
Days 37-39	The willingness to pay the price

Our lives are out of balance. We are too quickly absorbed, enthralled, and swept away by the fads of the day.

Step Two is a reminder that we can move toward wholeness in our lives by striving for a balanced perspective.

Reading for days 15, 16, 17 and 18

When I was a child, my speech, feelings and thinking were all those of a child; now that I am an adult, *I have no more use for childish ways.* What we see now is like a dim image in a mirror; then we shall see face-to-face. *What I know now is only partial;* then it will be as complete as God's knowledge of me.

You will learn the truth and the *truth will make you free.* So if the *Son makes you free*, you will be free indeed.

When Christ freed us, he meant us to *remain free.* Stand firm, therefore, and do not submit again to the yoke of slavery.

Patience, too, will have its practical results so that you *will become fully-developed, complete with nothing missing.*

The Spirit brings love, joy, peace, patience, kindness, goodness, trustfulness, gentleness and self control.

Based on I Corinthians 13:11-14; John 8:32; Galatians 5:1; James 1:4; Gal 5:22 (TEV and JB)

PERSONAL REFLECTIONS

Striving for a balanced perspective

<u>Day 15</u> (Be sure to make daily entries on the chart on page 100.)

Number of times the passage was read: _____

Today, I realized that my life is in process, moving towards completion and wholeness. I sought today to rid myself of one of my "childish" tendencies.

Degree to which I applied the passage to my life today: _____

<u>Day 16</u>

Number of times the passage was read: _____

Today, I acknowledged that enslavement and bondage prevent the natural flow towards completeness and a balanced life. Jesus Christ has set me free from this bondage. He gives me lasting freedom. In his power, I made a firm decision today to avoid those things that might enslave me again.

Degree to which I applied the passage to my life today: _____

Day 17

Number of times the passage was read: _____

Wholeness can be measured in part by the degree to which the fruits of the Holy Spirit are granted expression in my life. Today, I evaluated myself:

- *as one who loves;*
- *as one who brings joy to others;*
- *as one who brings goodness;*
- *as one who is patient;*
- *as one who is kind;*
- *as one who is trusting;*
- *as one who is faithful;*
- *as one who is gentle;*
- *as one who is self-controlled.*

Rate yourself as 1-10 on each fruit of the Spirit.

Degree to which I applied the passage to my life today (average of the above) :_____

Day 18

Number of times the passage was read: _____

Today, I recognized that the balanced perspective will be reached by keeping my eyes on the person of Jesus Christ. I asked for his help in avoiding all other issues, circumstances, problems, or theologies that would seek to take my eyes off him, my center and balancing point.

Degree to which I applied the passage to my life today:_____

It is love that inspires and motivates. Love is what we seek. Love is what we seek to give.

A person, "a power greater than ourselves, who came in the person of Jesus Christ came to transform our weaknesses into strengths."

Reading for days 19, 20, and 21

Dear friends, *let us love one another,* because love comes from God. Whoever loves is a child of God and knows God. Whoever does not love does not know God, for God is love. And *God showed love for us by sending Jesus Christ into the world, so that we might have life through him.* This is what love is: it is not that we have loved God, but that God loved us and sent Christ to be the means by which our sins are forgiven.

Dear brothers and sisters, if this is how God loved us, then we should love one another. No one has ever seen God, but if we love one another, God lives in union with us, and God's love is made perfect in us. We are sure that we live in union with God because we have been given the Spirit. And we have seen and tell others that God sent Jesus Christ to be the Savior of the world. If anyone declares that Jesus is the Son of God, that person lives in union with God and God lives in union with that person. And we ourselves know and believe the love which God has for us. God is love, and whoever lives in love lives in union with God and God lives in union with that person. Love is made perfect in us in order that we may have courage on the Judgment Day; and we will have it because our life in this world is the same as Christ's. There is no fear in love; perfect love drives out all fear. So then, love has not been made perfect in anyone who is afraid, because fear has to do with punishment. We love because God first loved us. If you say you love God but hate your brother or sister, you are a liar. For you cannot love God, whom you have not seen, if you do not love your brother or sister, whom you have seen. The command that Christ has given us is this: if you love God you must also love your brothers and sisters.

There is no need to write you about love for your fellow believers. You yourselves have been taught by God how you should love one another.
Based on 1 John 4:7-21; 1 Thessalonians 4:9 (TEV and JB)

PERSONAL REFLECTIONS

Receiving and giving love

Day 19

Number of times the passage was read: _____

Today, I recognized that God loves me and showed it by sending Jesus Christ to lay down his life for me. For this, I gave thanks in a variety of ways.

Degree to which I applied the passage to my life today: _____

Day 20

Number of times the passage was read: _____

Today, I acknowledged my need for love. I know that I must be loved first, before I can love others. By living in union with God and my brothers and sisters, my needs will be met so that I will be set free to love others.

Degree to which I applied the passage to my life today: _____

Day 21

Number of times the passage was read: _____

Today, I made a decision to love others. I will especially support those who follow Christ.

Degree to which I applied the passage to my life today: _____

This person, "a power greater than ourselves," can be experienced in numerous ways.

Daily prayer and meditation are crucial for those who seek personal growth and development.

Reading for days 22, 23, and 24

"The greatest thing anyone can do for God and man is pray. It is not the only thing but it is the chief thing. The great people of the earth today are the people who pray. I do not mean those who talk about prayer, nor those who say they believe in prayer, nor yet those who can explain about prayer, but I mean those people who take time to pray."

-S.D. Gordon

SERENITY PRAYER

God, grant me the serenity to accept the things I cannot change; courage to change the things I can and wisdom to know the difference, living one day at a time, enjoying one moment at a time, accepting hardship as a pathway to peace, taking as Jesus did, this sinful world as it is, not as I would have it, trusting that you will make all things right if I surrender to Your will, so that I may be reasonably happy in this life and supremely happy with You forever in the next.

-Rienhold Neibuhr

(Reading continued on next page)

Ask, and you will receive; seek, and you will find; knock, and the door will be opened to you. The one who asks will receive, and anyone who seeks will find, and the door will be opened to the person who knocks.

There is no need to worry; *if there is anything you need, pray for it,* asking God for it with prayer and thanksgiving and that peace of God, which is so much greater than we can understand, will guard your hearts and minds in Christ Jesus.

If any of you lacks wisdom, you should pray to God, who will give it to you; because God gives generously and graciously to all. But when you pray, you must believe and not doubt at all. Whoever doubts is like a wave in the sea that is driven and blown about by the wind.

I urge that petitions, prayers, requests and thanksgiving be offered to God for all people; for kings and all others who are in authority, that we may live a quiet and peaceful life with all reverence toward God and with proper conduct. This is good and it pleases God our Savior, who wants everyone to be saved and to come to know the truth. For there is one God, and there is one who brings God and humanity together: the man Jesus Christ.

If you abide in me and my words remain in you, you may ask what you will and you shall get it.

Pray constantly.

There, he (Daniel) knelt down at the open windows and *prayed to God three times a day.*

Very *early, long before daylight,* Jesus got up and left the house. He went out to a lonely place, where he prayed.

Do all this in prayer, asking for God's help. *Pray on every occasion as the Spirit leads.* For this reason keep alert and never give up; pray always for all of God's people.

The Spirit also comes to help us pray, weak as we are. For we don't know how we ought to pray; the Spirit pleads with God for us in groans that words cannot express. And God, who sees into our hearts, knows what the thought of the Spirit is; because the Spirit pleads with God on behalf of God's people and in accordance with God's will.

Based on Matthew 7:7-9; Phillipians 4:6-7; James 1:5; 1 Timothy 2:1-6; John 15:7; I Thess. 5:17; Hebrews 4:16; Daniel 5:11; Luke 4:42; Romans 8:26-27 (TEV and JB)

PERSONAL REFLECTIONS

The importance of daily prayer and meditation

Day 22

Number of times the passage was read: _____

Today, I made a decision to develop the habit of prayer. This habit of prayer will replace the habit of worry.

Degree to which I applied the passage to my life today: _____

Day 23

Number of times the passage was read: _____

Today, I determined to become a consistent prayer person. I will establish a specific time and place for prayer each day. I will discipline myself to follow through on my plan.

Degree to which I applied the passage to my life today: _____

Day 24

Number of times the passage was read: _____

Today, I recognized that I do not know how to pray. I was relieved to discover that I do not have to be "good" at prayer. The Spirit will plead with God through and for me. All that is needed is my availability and my willingness to give the Spirit access to my life.

Degree to which I applied the passage to my life today: _____

The expression of gratitude brings health and wholeness.

I am grateful today, that I have "come to believe".

Step Two is a reminder that the ability to believe is a gift. For that gift, we give thanks.

Reading for days 25 and 26

Sing to God with thanksgiving in your heart. Everything you do or say should be done in the name of the Lord Jesus as you give thanks through him to God.

Now on the way to Jerusalem he traveled along the border between Samaria and Galilee. As he entered one of the villages, ten lepers came to meet him. They stood some way off and called to him, "Jesus, Master, take pity on us." When he saw them he said, "Go and show yourselves to the priests." Now as they were going away they were cleansed. *Finding himself cured*, one of them turned back praising God at the top of his lungs and threw himself at the feet of Jesus and thanked him. The man was a Samaritan. This made Jesus say, "Were not all ten made clean? The other nine, where are they? It seems that no one has come back to give praise to God, except this foreigner." And he said to the man, "Stand up and go on your way. Your faith has saved you."

I will proclaim Your greatness, my Lord and King; I will thank you forever and ever. Every day I will thank you; I will praise You forever and ever. The Lord is great and is to be highly praised; God's What you have done will be praised from one generation to the next; they will proclaim your mighty acts.

I will meditate on your wonderful deeds. I will proclaim your greatness.

The Lord is loving and merciful, slow to become angry and full of constant love.

(Reading continued on next page)

God is good to everyone and has compassion on all.
All your creatures, Lord, will praise you, and all your people will give you thanks.
God helps those who are in trouble; those who have fallen are lifted up.
All living things look hopefully to you, and you give them food when they need it.

You give them enough and satisfy the needs of all.
You are near to those who call to you, who call to you with sincerity.

God supplies the needs of those who honor the Lord; their cries are heard and they are saved.

All who love the Lord are protected. I will always praise the Lord; let all creatures praise the Lord forever.

Based on Colossians 3:16-17; Luke 17:11-19; Psalm 145 (TEV and JB)

PERSONAL REFLECTIONS

Expressing gratitude

<u>Day 25</u>

Number of times the passage was read: _____

Like the cleansed leper, today I returned to Jesus Christ to give thanks for his cleansing work in my life.

Degree to which I applied the passage to my life today: _____

<u>Day 26</u>

Number of times the passage was read: _____

Like David, the psalmist, I sought today to give praise and thanksgiving to God. This is something I will seek to do at the beginning and end of each day.

Degree to which I applied the passage to my life today: _____

We find our wholeness in this one, Jesus Christ,
"who is greater than ourselves."

Reading for days 27, 28, 29, 30, and 31

This is an awesome thought...
that all fulfillment in life is found in a person, in God, as expressed in Jesus Christ.

All through history, many have affirmed this truth. In our present day, almost 2000 years after his life, death and resurrection, multitudes continue to maintain that their fulfillment is in the person of Jesus Christ.

(Reading continued on next page)

ONE SOLITARY LIFE

Here is a man who was born in an obscure village... the child of a peasant woman. He grew up in another obscure village... he worked in a carpenter shop until he was thirty... and then for three years he was an itinerant preacher.

He never wrote a book... he never held an office... he never owned a home... he never had a family... he never went to college... he never put his foot inside a big city... he never traveled more than two hundred miles from the place where he was born... he never did one of the things that usually accompany greatness... he had no credentials but himself... he had nothing to do with this world except the naked power of his divine manhood... While still a young man, the tide of popular opinion turned against him... his friends ran away... One of them denied him... he was turned over to his enemies... he went through the mockery of a trial... he was nailed to a cross between two thieves... his executioners gambled for the only piece of property he had on earth while he was dying... and that was his coat.

When he was dead, he was taken down and laid in a borrowed grave through the pity of a friend.

Nineteen centuries have come and gone and today he is the centerpiece of the human race and the leader of the column of progress.

I am far within the mark when I say that all the armies that ever marched... and all the navies that were built... and all the parliaments that ever sat, and all the kings that ever reigned put together have not affected the life of people upon this earth as powerfully as has that One Solitary Life. -- author unknown

Jesus says, *I have come to bring you life,* life in all its fullness.

I am the way, the truth, and the life;
no one goes to God except by me.

For the full divinity of God lives in Christ in his humanity, and you *have been given full life in union with him. He is supreme over every spiritual ruler and authority.*

Jesus Christ is the visible expression of the invisible God. He is the first Son, superior to all created things. Through him God created everything in heaven and on earth, the seen and the unseen things, including spiritual powers, lords, rulers, and authorities. God created the whole universe through him and for him. Christ existed before all things, and *in union with him all things have their proper place.* He is the head of his body, the church; *he is the source of the body's life.* Through the Son, the whole universe was brought back to God. God made peace through Christ's death on the cross and so brought back all things.

But God raised Jesus high and gave him the name which is *above* all other names that all beings in the heavens, on earth and in the underworld should bend the knee at the name of Jesus and that every tongue should acclaim Jesus Christ as Lord, to the glory of God.

Jesus cried out, If anyone is thirsty, let that one come to Me. Let the person come and drink who believes in Me.

(Reading continued on next page)

Then Jesus turned to the disciples and said to them privately, *"How fortunate you are to see the things you see.* I know that many prophets and kings wanted to see what you see but they could not, and to hear what you hear, but they did not."

... I know nothing can happen that will outweigh the supreme advantage of knowing Christ Jesus my Lord. For him I have accepted the loss of everything and I look on everything as garbage if only I can have Christ and be given a place in him. *I am no longer trying for perfection by my own efforts,* the perfection that comes through the law, but I want only the perfection that comes through faith in Christ and is from God and based on faith. *All I want is to know Christ and the power of his resurrection....*

Based on John 10:10; 14:6; Colossians 2:9-10; 1:15-20; Phillipians 2:9-11; John 7:37-39; Luke 10:23-24; Phillipians 3:8-10 (TEV and JB)

PERSONAL REFLECTIONS

Finding wholeness in the person of Jesus Christ

<u>Day 27</u>

Number of times the passage was read: _____

Today, I acknowledged that Jesus Christ came to bring the abundant, full, rich life to me.

Degree to which I applied the passage to my life today: _____

<u>Day 28</u>

Number of times the passage was read: _____

Everything was created through and for Jesus Christ. This is almost impossible to comprehend. In union with him, I will find my place in life. In union with him, I have everything that I need.

Degree to which I applied the passage to my life today: _____

<u>Day 29</u>

Number of times the passage was read: _____

The name Jesus Christ is the name above all names. His name is powerful. I want to use his name reverently and frequently.

Degree to which I applied the passage to my life today: _____

Reading for days 27-31 (continued)

One day Jesus got into a boat with his disciples and said to them, "Let us go across to the other side of the lake."
They began their journey.
As they were sailing, Jesus fell asleep. Suddenly a strong wind blew down on the lake, and the boat began to fill with water, so that they were all in great danger. The disciples went to Jesus and woke him up, saying, "Master, Master, we are about to die." Jesus got up and gave an order to the wind and to the stormy water; they quieted down, and there was a great calm. Then he said to the disciples, "Where is your faith?" But they were amazed and afraid, and said to one another, *"Who is this person? He gives orders to the wind and waves, and they obey him."*

Jesus said,
No one can be the slave of two masters; he will hate one and love the other; he will be faithful to one and despise the other. You cannot serve both God and money.

Based on Luke 8:22-25; Matthew 6:24 (TEV)

Day 30

Number of times the passage was read: _____

Today, I see Jesus not only as Savior, Friend and Creator... today, I see him as Master and Lord of my life.

Degree to which I applied the passage to my life today: _____

Day 31

Number of times the passage was read: _____

Today, I sought to commit myself to the Lordship of Jesus Christ. I want to serve him and him alone. I don't want any other "false gods" to come between us. I asked for his help and laid before him those things which distract me .

Degree to which I applied the passage to my life today: _____

Step Two of the Twelve Steps is a reminder that Jesus Christ can transform our weaknesses into strengths. Some of this transformation takes place when we extend ourselves to others.

By reaching out and sharing, I move closer to a balanced life.

Reading for days 32 and 33

Jesus says,
The greatest love you can have for your friends is to give your life for them.

Jesus says,
I give you a new commandment: *love one another;* just as I have loved you, you also must love one another. By this love you have for one another, everyone will know that you are my followers.

This is how we know what love is: Christ gave his life for us. We too, then, ought to give our lives for our brothers and sisters.

Look out for each other's interests. The attitude you should have is the one that Jesus Christ had: his state was divine, yet he did not cling to his equality with God, but emptied himself to become as human beings and having taken on flesh, he was humbler yet, even to accepting death, death on a cross. But God raised him high and gave him the name which is above all names, so that all beings in the heavens, the earth and the underworld, should bend their knee at the name of Jesus and openly acclaim that Jesus Christ is Lord to the glory of God.

Based on John 15:13; 13:34-45; 1 John 3:16; Phillipians 2:4-11 (TEV and JB)

PERSONAL REFLECTIONS

Extending yourself to another

Day 32

Number of times the passage was read: _____

Today, I made up my mind to serve others by loving them. I want to do what is best for them without expecting anything in return.

Degree to which I applied the passage to my life today: _____

Day 33

Number of times the passage was read: _____

Today, I realized that I can serve others by looking out for their interests and needs. I freely choose to give myself to others.

Degree to which I applied the passage to my life today: _____

Jesus Christ can transform my weaknesses into strengths.

I, for my part, can cooperate in the transformation by being teachable... I am a student, a life long student. Significant growth will take place because I see myself in the process of learning and growing.

Reading for days 34 and 35

Christ's message in all its richness must live in your hearts. *Teach and instruct* one another with all wisdom.

I study your instructions; I examine your teachings. I take pleasure in your laws; your commands I will not forget. *I will study your teachings.* Your instructions give me pleasure; they are my advisors. Help me to understand your laws, and I will meditate on your wonderful teachings. Teach me, Lord, the meaning of your laws, and I will obey them at all times. I will meditate on your instructions. Your Word is a lamp to guide me and a light for my path. All night long I lie awake, to meditate on your Word.

The Word of God is something alive and active.

Be sure that the Book of the Law is always on your lips. Study it day and night, and make sure that you obey everything written in it. Then you will be prosperous and successful.

Since you have accepted Christ Jesus as Lord, *live in union with him.* Keep your roots deep in him, build your lives on him, and become stronger in faith, as you were taught.

Based on Colossians 3:16a; Psalm 119:15-16; 18; 23-24; 27; 33; 48; 73; 105; 148; Hebrews 4:12; Joshua 1:8; Colossians 2:6-10 (TEV and JB)

PERSONAL REFLECTIONS

Seeing yourself as a student

Day 34

Number of times the passage was read: _____

Today, Lord, I acknowledge my desire to see the truths contained in your Word. I want to study your teachings. I want to grow in my respect for your commands. I know that your Word is a lamp to guide me and a light for my path.

Degree to which I applied the passage to my life today: _____

Day 35

Number of times the passage was read: _____

I want to become stronger in my faith, Lord. This will happen as I study your Word and make it more a part of me. Help me, Lord, to study what you have revealed about yourself. Today, I want to establish a "system" for daily study of your Word.

Degree to which I applied the passage to my life today: _____

... and while I am a student, I am at the same time a teacher. I have much to share with others. That I have something to give to others is more evidence that my weaknesses are being transformed into strengths.

Reading for day 36

My brothers and sisters,
be strong through the grace that is ours in union with Christ Jesus. *Take the teachings* that you have heard me teach and *entrust them to reliable people who will be able to teach others also.* Take your part in suffering, as a loyal follower of Christ Jesus.

Be one who correctly teaches the message of God's truth.

Based on II Timothy 2:1-7;15 (TEV)

PERSONAL REFLECTIONS

Seeing yourself as a teacher

Day 36

Number of times the passage was read: _____

Today, I made a decision to share with others what I have to give. In this process, I recognized my need to grow strong and share the teachings that have been given to me.

Degree to which I applied the passage to my life today: _____

I want to grow. Step Two reminds me that I can grow and become whole. I want to be transformed. I am willing to pay the price, whatever it may be, so that I can become healthy, whole, balanced.

Reading for days 37, 38, and 39

You deserve congratulations when you are persecuted because you are doing what God requires.

Jesus said,
A servant is not greater than his master. If they persecuted me, they will persecute you too.

My brothers and sisters, *you will always have your trials*, but when they come, try to treat them as a happy privilege. You understand that your faith is only put to the test to make you patient, but patience too is to have its practical results so that you will become *fully-developed, complete, with nothing missing.*

During his life on earth, Jesus offered up prayers aloud and in silent tears, to the One who had the power to save him out of death, and he submitted so humbly that his prayer was heard.

Be glad about these trials, even though it may now be necessary for you to be sad for a while. Their purpose is to prove that your faith is genuine. Even gold, which can be destroyed, is tested by fire; and so your faith, which is much more precious than gold, must also be tested, so that it may endure. Then you will receive praise and glory and honor on the day when Jesus Christ returns.

Every trial that you have experienced is the kind that normally comes to people. God keeps this promise, and you will not be tested beyond your power to remain firm; at the time you are put to the test, you will be given the strength to endure it, and you will also be given a way out.

We know that all things work together for good for the ones who love God.

If you endure suffering even when you have done right, God will bless you for it. It was to this that God called you, for Christ himself suffered for you and left you an example, so that you would follow in his steps. He committed no sin, and no one ever heard a lie come from his lips. When he was insulted, he did not answer back with an insult; when he suffered, he did not threaten but *placed his hopes in God, the Righteous Judge.*

Everything that was written long ago in the Scriptures was meant to teach us something about hope. *People who did not give up were helped by God.*

I know what it's like to be in need and what it's like to have more than enough. I have learned this secret, so that anywhere, at any time, I am content, whether I am full or hungry, whether I have too much or too little. I have strength to face all conditions by the power that Christ gives me.

To have faith is to be sure of the things that we hope for, to be certain of the things we cannot see. It was faith that made Noah hear God's warning about things in the future that he could not see. It was by faith that Abraham had the courage to leave his home, not knowing God's intended destination. Isaac and Jacob also had faith, as did Sarah, who became a mother at a very old age. What a record all of these have won by their faith. Yet they did not receive what God had promised because God had decided on an even better plan for us.

Based on Matthew 5:10-12; John 15:20; James 1:2-4; Hebrews 5:7; I Peter 1:6-7; Luke 9:23-24; I Corinthians 10:13; Romans 8:28; I Peter 2:20-23; Matthew 5:11-12; Romans 15:4; Phillipians 4:12-13; Hebrews 11 (TEV and JB)

PERSONAL REFLECTIONS

The willingness to pay the price

Day 37

Number of times the passage was read: _____

Today, I realized it may be costly to become whole. But whatever the price, I will pay it.

Degree to which I applied the passage to my life today: _____

Day 38

Number of times the passage was read: _____

Today, I decided, that even when I am tired, I will not give up. I will learn to be content with what I have, no matter what the circumstances are.

Degree to which I applied the passage to my life today: _____

Day 39

Number of times the passage was read: _____

Today, I made a decision to anticipate and embrace the suffering, setbacks and discouragements I could be confronted with in my lifetime. When trials, struggles and sadness come, I will embrace them.

Degree to which I applied the passage to my life today: _____

EVALUATION CHART

How balanced is my life becoming?

+ Today my life was centered and balanced
0 Today I leaned too intensely into one dimension of life
- Today my life was without balance

	Day	
	15 16 17 18 19 20 21 22 23 24 25 26 27 28 29 30 31 32 33 34 35 36 37 38 39	
		10
	+	9
		8
		7
		6
	0	5
		4
		3
	-	2
		1

STEP THREE

We make a decision to turn our will and our lives over to the care of Jesus Christ as we understand Him, hoping to understand Him more fully.

Day 40	The importance of taking care of myself
Days 41-45	The importance of relationships
Days 46-48	The importance of being involved with others who can give support
Day 49	The importance of extending yourself

We have the ability, the power to make a decision to turn our wills and our lives over to the care of Christ. To turn our wills, our minds, and our decision-making faculties over to the care of Christ means we choose to let him love us and express himself to us.

When we decide to turn our lives over to the care of Christ, we turn over not only our wills, but our very lives. This includes our feelings, health, future, present, struggles, relationships, ideas, resources, gifts... everything.

He not only wants to care for our wills, he also wants to express his love and concern for every dimension of our lives.

"... as we understand him." Perhaps we don't know him well enough to know that he can be trusted.... that he does care for us just as we are. When we trust him with where we are right now, at the moment, he gives us the ability to trust him even more. It is true that "we can cast all our worries upon him because he is looking after us."

Part of turning our will and our lives over to the care of Christ is learning the importance of taking care of myself.

Reading for day 40

When anyone is joined to Christ, that person is a new creation; the old has gone, and the new has come.

Jesus called out in a loud voice, "Lazarus, come out!" He came out, his hands and feet wrapped in grave cloths, and with a cloth around his face. "Untie him," Jesus told them, "and let him go."

Based on II Corinthians 5:17 and John 11:43 (TEV)

PERSONAL REFLECTIONS

The importance of taking care of myself

Day 40 (Be sure to make daily entries on the chart on page 126.)

Number of times the passage was read: _____

Today, I recognized that I am a new creation. This "new me" needs to be cared for. I will do what I must to be sure that I am refreshed. Today, I made decisions and arrangements for this renewal to take place on a continuous basis.

Degree to which I applied the passage to my life today: _____

Another dimension of turning our will and lives over to the care of Christ is developing relationships.

These relationships, especially in our families, are crucial to our own personal growth and development.

Reading for days 41, 42, 43, 44, and 45

For God loved the world so much that *he gave his only son*, so that whoever believes in him will not die but have eternal life.

Because of our love for you, we were ready to share with you not only the Good News about Christ, but even our own lives. You were so dear to us.

The word was made flesh, and *he lived with us*, and we saw his glory, the glory that is his as the only Son of God, full of grace and truth.

Based on John 3:16; I Thessalonians 2:8; John 1:14 (TEV and JB)

PERSONAL REFLECTIONS

The importance of relationships

<u>Day 41</u>

Number of times the passage was read: _____

Today, I acknowledged that God desires a relationship with me and I assessed my own desire to have a relationship with God.

Degree to which I applied the passage to my life today: _____

<u>Day 42</u>

Number of times the passage was read: _____

Today, I expressed gratitude for the relationships in my life. I realized that they are very important to me.

Degree to which I applied the passage to my life today: _____

<u>Day 43</u>

Number of times the passage was read: _____

Today, I made a decision to put more emphasis on those important relationships in my life. I will do something to encourage them.

Degree to which I applied the passage to my life today: _____

Reading for days 41-45 (continued)

Give way to one another in obedience to Christ.

...husbands should love their wives just as Christ loved the church and sacrificed himself for her to make her holy. He made her clean by washing her in water with a form of words, so that when he took her to himself she would be glorious, with no speck or wrinkle or anything like that, but holy and faultless.

In the same way, husbands must love their wives just as they love their own bodies; for a man to love his wife is for him to love himself.

A man never hates his own body; but he feeds it and looks after it; and that is the way Christ treats the church, because it is his body and we are its living parts.

For this reason, a man must leave his father and mother and be joined to his wife, and the two will become one body. This mystery has many implications.

To sum up, each one of you must love your wife as you love yourself; and let every wife respect her husband.

Children, be obedient to your parents in the Lord, that is your duty. The first commandment that has a promise attached to it is: Honor your father and mother and you will prosper and have a long life in the land.

Parents, never drive your children to resentment but, in bringing them up correctly, guide them as the Lord does.

Based on Ephesians 5:21-6:4 (JB)

Day 44

Number of times the passage was read: _____

Today, I made a decision to make my family the priority in my life. This will be reflected in my schedule... in the amount of time I spend with them.

Degree to which I applied the passage to my life today: _____

Day 45

Number of times the passage was read: _____

Today, I did something tangible to express my love for my family, especially my parents.

Degree to which I applied the passage to my life today: _____

Turning my will and my life over to the care of Jesus Christ will also mean gathering with others who can support me as I seek to live a life in him.

Reading for days 46, 47, and 48

Jesus said,
Don't be afraid. *Go and tell my brothers and sisters to go to Galilee and there they will see me.*

You must not be called "teacher" because you are all brothers and sisters of one another and have only one Teacher.

Jesus said,
I have prayed for you, Simon, that your faith will not fail. And when you turn back to me *you must strengthen your brothers and sisters.*

The trials that you have had to bear are *no more than people normally have.* You can trust God. You will not be tried beyond your strength. With any trial you will be given a way out of it and the strength to bear it.

When the right time finally came, God sent Jesus Christ. He came as the son of a human mother and lived under the Jewish Law to save those who were under the Law, so that we might become God's children. To show you are God's children, the spirit of Christ was sent into your hearts. So then, you are no longer a slave but a child. *And since you are God's child, you will be given all that God has for you.*

Jesus says,
Love one another. As I have loved you, so you must love one another. If you have love for one another, then everyone will know that you are my disciples.

(Reading continued on next page)

....go and *be reconciled with your brother or sister,* and then come back to the altar and present your offering.

If your brother or sister does something wrong, go and have it out between yourselves. If he/she listens to you, you have won that person back. If she/he does not listen, take one or two others along with you: the evidence of two or three witnesses is required to sustain any charge. But if she/he refuses to listen to these, report it to the community and if he/she refuses to listen to the community, treat her/him like a pagan or a tax collector.

Let us be concerned for one another, to help one another to show love and to do good. Let us not give up the habit of meeting together.... let us encourage one another all the more since you see that the day of the Lord is coming nearer.

By speaking the truth in love, we must grow up in every way to Christ, who is the head.

Jesus prayed,
May they all be one. May they be one in us, as you are in me and I am in you, so that the world may believe it was you who sent me.

The whole group of believers was united in heart and soul.

Brothers and sisters, we wish you happiness; try to grow perfect; help one another. Be united; live in peace, and the God of love and peace will be with you.

(Reading continued on next page)

Be united in your convictions and united in your love with a common purpose and a common mind.

If any of the saints are in need you must share with them; and you should make hospitality your special care.

You are citizens, like all the saints, and part of God's household. You are part of a building that has the apostles and prophets for its foundation, and Christ Jesus Himself for its cornerstone. As every structure is aligned on him, all grow into one holy temple in the Lord; and you too are being built into a house where God lives, in the Spirit.

Just as a human body, though it is made up of many parts, is a single unit because all these parts, though many, make one, so it is with Christ. God put all the separate parts into the body on purpose. You together are Christ's body; but each of you is a different part of it.

Based on Matthew 28:10; Luke 22:32; 1 Corinthians 10:13; Galatians 4:4-7; John 13:34-35; Matthew 5:22-24; Matthew 18:15-17; Hebrews 10:24-25; Ephesians 4:15; John 17:21; Acts 4:32; II Corinthians 13:11; Phillipians 2:2a; Romans 12:13; Ephesians 2:19-22; I Corinthians 12:12-30 (TEV and JB)

PERSONAL REFLECTIONS

The importance of being involved with others who can give support

Day 46

Number of times the passage was read: _____

Today, I acknowledged my need for brothers and sisters in my life. These are friends that I will share with and be strengthened by. Today, I will give them one more part of myself. I will trust them.

Degree to which I applied the passage to my life today: _____

Day 47

Number of times the passage was read: _____

Today, I experienced a little bit more of what it is like to be a child of God. I realized some of the benefits of being God's child. I also acknowledged that as God's child, I will have trials to bear.

Degree to which I applied the passage to my life today: _____

Day 48

Number of times the passage was read: _____

Today, I gave the thanks for the body of Christ, the church. As I reflected on this awesome and powerful body, I was reminded of God's abiding presence and power working in and through the church through the years. I made a decision to become an active member of my own congregation. This commitment I made knowing that God has put me there to exercise my individual gifts in order to strengthen the whole body of Christ.

Degree to which I applied the passage to my life today: _____

An important part of turning our lives over to the care of Christ is our willingness to open ourselves to those who are hurting so that his care for them might be expressed through us.

Reading for day 49

When anyone is joined to Christ, that person is a new being; the old has gone, the new has come. All this is done by God; through Christ we were changed into God's friends and were given the task of making others God's friends also. Our message is that God was making friends of all humanity through Christ. God did not keep an account of their sins, and we have been given the message which tells how all of humanity is made friends with God. Here we are then, speaking for Christ, *as though God were making an appeal through us.* We plead on Christ's behalf: let God be your friend. Christ was without sin, but for our sake God made him share our sin in order that in union with him we might share the righteousness of God.

Something which has existed since the beginning, that we have heard, and we have seen with our own eyes; that we have watched and touched with our hands: the word, who is life, this is our subject. That life was made visible: we saw it and we are giving our testimony, telling you of the eternal life which was with God and has been made visible to us. *What we have seen and heard we are telling you so that you to may be in union with us,* as we are in union with God and Jesus Christ.

Based on II Corinthians 5:17-21; 1 John 1:1-4 (TEV and JB)

PERSONAL REFLECTIONS

The importance of extending yourself

Day 49

Number of times the passage was read: _____

Today, I realized that God, through Christ, changed me from an enemy into a friend. I have now been given the privilege of making others God's friends also. My own joy is complete when I share myself and my awareness of Christ's love with others.

Degree to which I applied the passage to my life today: _____

EVALUATION CHART

How well am I doing in turning my will and life over to the care of Christ?

+ Today I turned my will and my life over to the care of Jesus Christ
0 Today I reluctantly turned my will and my life over to the care of Jesus Christ
- Today I withheld myself from Christ and most of the other people I encountered

	Day	
40 41 42 43 44 45 46 47 48 49		10
+		9
		8
		7
		6
0		5
		4
		3
-		2
		1

STEP FOUR

We make a searching and fearless moral inventory of both our strengths and weaknesses.

Days 50-52	You need something to live for, a vision that is your own
Days 53-54	Appreciating your own uniqueness
Days 55-56	Pressing for the full use of your potential
Days 57-59	Seeking out and exercising your gifts and talents
Days 60-61	Being positive
Days 62-64	Having clear, attainable, measurable goals
Days 65-67	Learning to be persistent
Day 68	Responding to the vision I am given
Days 69-70	The standard of excellence

The idea of doing a personal inventory seems tedious to most people. To some people the idea is threatening.

The inventory we are suggesting is primarily a positive venture. The readings and exercises on the following pages concentrate on the vision and strengths that you have within you.

Each person needs something to live for... a vision. These exercises will help you identify and clarify your own vision.

....an "inventory... of both our strengths and weaknesses."

You need something to live for... a vision that is your own.

Reading for days 50, 51, and 52

The Scriptures say, What no one ever saw or heard, *what no one ever thought could happen,* is the very thing that was prepared for those who love God.

Jesus said to them, For people this is impossible; *for God everything is possible.*

Jesus says, I tell you seriously, if your faith were the size of a mustard seed you could say to this mountain, move from here to here, and it would move; nothing would be impossible for you.

In particular, I urge you not to go on living the aimless kind of life that pagans live.

Jesus says, I am telling you the truth: whoever believes in me will do what I do, yes, *that person will do even greater things,* because I am going to God. And I will do whatever you ask for in my name so that God's glory will be shown through the Son. If you ask me for anything in my name, I will do it.

The Lord gave me (Habbakuk) this answer: *Write down clearly* on tablets what I reveal to you, so that it can be read at a glance. Put it in writing, because it is not yet time for it to come true. But the time is coming quickly, and what I show you will come true. It may seem a bit slow in coming, but wait for it; *it will most certainly take place,* and it will not be delayed.

(Reading continued on next page)

I alone know the plans I have for you, plans to bring prosperity and not disaster, plans to bring about the future you hope for.

Based on I Corinthians 2:9-10; Matthew 19:26; Matthew 17:20; Ephesians 4:17; John 14:12-14; Matthew 7:7-9; Habbakuk 2:2-3; Jeremiah 29:11 (TEV and JB)

PERSONAL REFLECTIONS

You need something to live for, a vision that is your own

Day 50 (Be sure to make daily entries on the chart on page 170.)

Number of times the passage was read: _____

Today, I recognized that God can and will do greater things than I could imagine. God can do the impossible.

Degree to which I applied the passage to my life today: _____

Day 51
Number of times the passage was read: _____

Today, I realized that those who trust in Jesus Christ can do some of what he did and even more.

Degree to which I applied the passage to my life today: _____

Day 52

Number of times the passage was read: _____

I believe clearer vision will come to me. When it does, I will write it down; refine it; read it often and let it develop within and through me.

Degree to which I applied the passage to my life today: _____

Appreciating your own uniqueness

Reading for days 53 and 54

You, Oh God, *created every part of me*; you put me together in my mother's womb. I praise you because you are to be feared; all you do is strange and wonderful. I know it with all my heart. When my bones were being formed, carefully put together in my mother's womb, when I was growing there in secret, you knew that I was there - you saw me before I was born.

The days allotted to me had all been recorded in your book, before any of them ever began.

People don't light a lamp and then hide it or put it under a bowl. Instead, they put it on the lampstand so that others may see the light as they come in.

Your eyes are like a lamp for the body. When your eyes are sound, your whole body is full of light; but when your eyes are no good, your whole body will be in darkness.

Based on Psalm 139:13-16; Luke 11:33-34
(TEV)

PERSONAL REFLECTIONS

Appreciating your own uniqueness

<u>Day 53</u>

Number of times the passage was read: _____

God created me. God knows me, knows where I've been, and knows where I'm going. Today I gave thanks for God's involvement in my unique life.

Degree to which I applied the passage to my life today: _____

<u>Day 54</u>

Number of times the passage was read: _____

Today, I enjoyed the gifts and talents that I have been given. I will use them without reservation.

Degree to which I applied the passage to my life today: _____

Part of taking my inventory is recognizing my potential and pressing for its full use in my life.

Reading for days 55 and 56

I ask God to give you power to be strong in your inner selves, and I pray that Christ will make his home in your hearts through faith.

I pray that you may have your roots and foundation in love so that you, together with all God's people, may have the power to understand how broad and long, how high and deep is Christ's love. May you come to know his love (although it can never be fully known) and so be completely filled with the very nature of God. *By means of God's power working in us, we are able to do so much more than we can ever ask for or even think of.*

Jesus says,
I am telling you the truth: whoever believes in me will do what I do, that one will do even greater things, because I am going to God. And I will do whatever you ask for in my name, so that the God's glory will be shown through the Son. If you ask me for anything in my name, I will do it.

I can do all things through Christ who strengthens me.

What no one ever saw or heard, what no one every thought could happen, is the very thing that was prepared for those who love God.

Based on Ephesians 3:16-20; John 14:12-14; Phillipians 4:13; 1 Corinthians 2:9 (TEV)

PERSONAL REFLECTIONS

Pressing for the full use of your potential

<u>Day 55</u>

Number of times the passage was read: _____

Today, with Christ living in me, I accepted the fact that I have unlimited potential. I am convinced that he is able to do in and through me much more than I could ever ask or imagine.

Degree to which I applied the passage to my life today: _____

<u>Day 56</u>

Number of times the passage was read: _____

I am convinced that, with the help and strength of Jesus Christ, anything can be mastered.

Degree to which I applied the passage to my life today: _____

Taking your inventory includes seeking out and exercising your gifts and talents.

In addition to natural gifts and talents, if you are like most people, you also have God-given spiritual gifts.

It is good to know about all of our gifts and talents.

Reading for days 57, 58, and 59

A LIST OF SOME OF THE GIFTS GOD HAS GIVEN...

1. The gift of God's love
2. The gift of Jesus Christ
3. The gift of eternal life
4. The gift of the Bible
5. The gift of gathering with others
6. The gift of the fruits of the Holy Spirit
7. The gift of being a founding leader/apostle
8. The gift of being a prophet
9. The gift of telling others about God
10. The gift of being a pastor
11. The gift of being a teacher
12. The gift of wisdom
13. The gift of knowledge
14. The gift of faith
15. The gift of healing
16. The gift of miraculous powers
17. The gift of discernment
18. The gift of speaking/praying in an unknown "prayer language"
19. The gift of interpreting an unknown language
20. The gift of helping others
21. The gift of administration
22. The gift of ministering to others
23. The gift of preaching
24. The gift of exhortation
25. The gift of alms-giving
26. The gift of mercy

(Reading continued on next page)

Each one of us has received a special gift according to what Christ has given.

The Spirit's presence is shown in some way in each person for the good of all.

Now instead of the spirit of the world, *we have received the Spirit that comes from God,* to teach us to understand the gifts that we have been given.

We love because God first loved us.

The testimony is this: *God has given us eternal life,* and this life has its source in the Son. Whoever has the Son has this life; whoever does not have the Son does not have life. This has been written to you so that you may know that you have eternal life.

For God loved the world so much that *he gave his only son,* so that whoever believes in him will not but have have eternal life.

All Scripture is inspired by God and can be used for teaching, for correcting error, for guiding people's lives and teaching them to be holy. This is how the person dedicated to God becomes fully equipped and ready to do ministry.

Something which has existed since the beginning, that we have heard, and *we have seen with our own eyes,* that we have watched and touched with our hands: The Word, who is life. That life was made visible: we saw it and we are giving our testimony, telling you of the eternal life which was with God and has been made visible to you.

(Reading continued on next page)

The Spirit brings the fruits of love, joy, peace, patience, kindness, goodness, trustfulness, gentleness and self control.

God will give the Holy Spirit to those who ask.

Fan into a flame the gift that God gave you when I laid my hands on you. God's gift is not a spirit of fear, but the Spirit of power, love and self-control.

Based on Ephesians 4:7; I Corinthians 12:7; 2:12; 1 John 4:19; 5:11-13; John 3:16; II Timothy 3:16-17; 1 John 1:1-4; Galatians 5:22; Luke 11:13; II Timothy 1:6-7; Ephesians 4:12

PERSONAL REFLECTIONS

Seeking out and exercising your gifts and talents

Day 57

Number of times the passage was read: _____

Today, I embraced the gift of eternal life given to me by Jesus Christ.

Degree to which I applied the passage to my life today: _____

Day 58

Number of times the passage was read: _____

Today, I gave thanks for the gift of the Bible. I see more clearly how it will equip me for life.

Degree to which I applied the passage to my life today: _____

Day 59

Number of times the passage was read: _____

Today, I gave thanks for the special spiritual gifts that have been given to me. I made a decision to make better use of them.

Degree to which I applied the passage to my life today: _____

Making the fourth step requires a positive attitude. There is no doubt about how much wrong we have done. We have limitations. Our weaknesses may be well known to us and perhaps others around us. By being positive, we can more easily identify our good points... our giftedness... our hopeful side.

Reading for days 60 and 61

My brothers and sisters,
fill your minds with those things that are good and that deserve praise:
things that are true,
noble,
right,
pure,
lovely,
and honorable.

Jesus went up a hill where he sat down.
His disciples gathered around him and he began to teach them:
Happy are those who know they are spiritually poor; the Kingdom of Heaven belongs to them.
Happy are those who mourn; God will comfort them.
Happy are those who are humble; they will receive what God has promised.
Happy are those whose greatest desire is to do what God requires; God will satisfy them fully.
Happy are those who are merciful to others; God will be merciful to them.
Happy are the pure in heart; they will see God.
Happy are those who work for peace; they will be God's children.
Happy are those who are persecuted because they do what God requires; the Kingdom of Heaven belongs to them.
Happy are you when people insult you and persecute you and tell all kinds of evil lies against you because you are my followers. Be happy and glad, for a great reward is kept for you in heaven. This is how the prophets who lived before you were persecuted.

Based on Phillipians 4:8; Matthew 5: 1-12 (TEV)

PERSONAL REFLECTIONS

Being positive

<u>Day 60</u>

Number of times the passage was read: _____

Today, I made a decision that I want to fill my mind with those things that are good. I will try to focus on others and the good in them. I will see the good in myself.

Degree to which I applied the passage to my life today: _____

<u>Day 61</u>

Number of times the passage was read: _____

Today, I took an inventory of my own inner joy and happiness. I used the passage to evaluate and give thanks for the God-given happiness I have.

Degree to which I applied the passage to my life today: _____

Having clear, attainable, measurable goals helps us in taking an accurate inventory.

Reading for days 62, 63, and 64

Jesus said,
I know where I came from and where I am going.

I can assure you my brothers and sisters, I am far from thinking that I have already won.
All I can say is that I forget the past and *I press ahead for what is still to come.*

Then Joshua said to them... How much more time will you waste before taking possession of the land which the Lord your God has given to you?

Based on John 8:14; Phillipians 3:13-14; Joshua 18:3 (JB)

PERSONAL REFLECTIONS

Having clear, attainable, measurable goals

Day 62

Number of times the passage was read: _____

Today, I reflected on my past and where I came from. I also looked ahead to what is still to come. I gave thanks for the present.

Degree to which I applied the passage to my life today: _____

Day 63

Number of times the passage was read: _____

Today, I renewed my desire to have clear, attainable, measurable goals. I took one more step toward developing a system for evaluating those goals.

Degree to which I applied the passage to my life today: _____

Day 64

Number of times the passage was read: _____

On this day, I made a decision to waste no more time. I will move forward with my ideas and goals. I will take "possession" of that territory which has been given to me.

Degree to which I applied the passage to my life today: _____

Part of "making it" in life is dependent upon my ability to persist. How persistent have I been?

Reading for days 65, 66, and 67

Everything that was written long ago in the Scriptures was meant to teach us something about hope from the examples the Scriptures give of how *people who did not give up were helped by God.*

Because Christ has been raised from death, we are *filled with a living hope. We look forward to the rich blessings that God keeps for us.* These gifts are kept for you in heaven, where they cannot decay or spoil or fade away. They are for you, who through faith are kept safe by God's power.

Be glad about this, even though it may now be necessary for you to be sad for a while because of the many kinds of trials you suffer.

Their purpose is to prove that your faith is genuine. Even gold, which can be destroyed, is tested by fire; and so your faith, which is much more precious than gold, must also be tested, so that it may endure.

Build up your strength in union with the Lord and by means of God's mighty power. Put on all the armor that God gives you, so that you will be able to stand up against the devil's evil tricks.

For we aren't fighting against human beings but against the wicked spiritual forces in the heavenly world, the rulers, authorities, and cosmic powers of this dark age. *So put on God's armor now!* Then when the evil day comes, you will be able to resist the enemy's attacks; and after fighting to the end, you will still hold your ground. So stand ready with truth as a belt tight around your waist, with righteousness as your breastplate, and as your shoes the readiness to announce the Good News of peace.

At all times carry faith as a shield; for with it you will be able to put out all the burning arrows shot by the Evil One. Accept salvation as a helmet and the word of God as the sword which the Spirit gives you. Do all this in prayer, asking for God's help. Pray on every occasion as the Spirit leads. For this reason *keep alert and never give up;* pray always for all God's people.

Be strong through the grace that is ours in union with Christ Jesus. Take your part in suffering, as a faithful follower of Christ Jesus.

Never give in; never admit defeat; keep on working at the Lord's work always, knowing that, in the Lord, you cannot be laboring in vain.

Based on Romans 15:4; 1 Peter 1:3-9; Ephesians 6:10-19; 2 Timothy 2:1,3; 1 Corinthians 15:58 (TEV and JB)

PERSONAL REFLECTIONS

Learning to be persistent

Day 65

Number of times the passage was read: _____

Today, I acknowledged the truth...that people who do not give up are helped by God.

Degree to which I applied the passage to my life today: _____

Day 66

Number of times the passage was read: _____

Today, I expressed gratitude for the fact that I have a living hope. This hope is based on Jesus Christ and the kingdom to come. It is an unfading, uncompromising hope that will give me strength to persist and endure.

Degree to which I applied the passage to my life today: _____

Day 67

Number of times the passage was read: _____

Today, I held on tight to the visions that have been given for my life. I recognized that my ideals will be attained even though darkness may presently surround me. I made a decision to be strong and take my part in suffering as a faithful follower of Jesus Christ.

Degree to which I applied the passage to my life today: _____

As part of my inventory, am I willing to look at how well I respond to the direction, vision, and ideas that are given to me?

Reading for day 68

My brothers and sisters,
what good is it for someone to say that they have
faith if their actions do not prove it? Can that
faith save that person? Suppose there are brothers
or sisters who need clothes and don't have enough
to eat. What good is there in your saying to them
"God bless you. Keep warm and eat well." if you
don't give them the necessities of life? So it is with
faith: if it is alone and includes no actions, then it
is dead.

We beg you once again not to neglect the grace of
God that you have received. For God says: At the
favorable time, I have listened to you; on the day
of salvation, I came to your help. Well, now is the
favorable time; this is the day of salvation.

Jesus said,
*Everyone who listens to these words of mine and
acts on them will be like a sensible* person who built
their house on a rock. Rain came down, floods rose,
gales blew and hurled themselves against that
house, and it did not fall: it was founded on rock.
But everyone who listens to these words of mine and
does not act on them will be like a stupid person
who built the house on sand. Rain came down,
floods rose, gales blew and struck that house and it
fell; and what a fall it had.

Based on James 2:14-20; II Corinthians 6:1-2;
Matthew 7:24-27

PERSONAL REFLECTIONS

Responding to the vision I am given

<u>Day 68</u>

Number of times the passage was read: _____

I will not hesitate another moment. I will put my faith into action. Now is the only time I have. This is the moment to act. I will take the next step necessary to implement the vision I believe I have been given.

Degree to which I applied the passage to my life today: _____

As I do my inventory, I will consider where I am in response to the ideal standard of excellence. This standard is not calling me to perfection. It is reminding me that I'll feel best about myself when I'm doing the best I can.

Reading for days 69 and 70

You have been raised to life with Jesus Christ, *so set your hearts on the things that are in heaven,* where Christ sits on the throne at the right side of God. Keep your minds fixed on things there, not on things here on earth. For you have died, and your life is hidden with Christ in God.

Fill your minds with everything that is true, noble, good, and pure, everything that we love, honor and everything that can be thought virtuous or worthy of praise.

Whatever you do, work at it with all your heart, as though you were working for the Lord and not for people.

Based on Colossians 3:1-3; Phillipians 4:8; Colossians 3:23

PERSONAL REFLECTIONS

The standard of excellence

<u>Day 69</u>

Number of times the passage was read: _____

As I focus on Christ and the heavenly perspective, I see him and his high standard for life. He wants me to do my best. I will seek to emulate his standard in my life, with his help.

Degree to which I applied the passage to my life today: _____

<u>Day 70</u>

Number of times the passage was read: _____

Today, I will use the words of Paul as standards for evaluation.... I seek to have my mind set on truth, nobility, goodness, purity, love, honor, virtue, and matters worthy of praise.

Degree to which I applied the passage to my life today: _____

EVALUATION CHART

My feelings toward and my response to my inventory

+ Today my vision was clear and I responded to it by enjoying myself and my gifts
0 Today I did not appreciate who I am and what I have to give to others
- Today I was negative, critical, and nonproductive

Day 50 51 52 53 54 55 56 57 58 59 60 61 62 63 64 65 66 67 68 69 70	
+	10
	9
	8
	7
	6
0	5
	4
	3
-	2
	1

Afterword

In the book of Isaiah it is written:
A voice cries out,
"proclaim a message!"
"What message am I to proclaim?" I (Isaiah) ask.
"Proclaim that all people are like grass;
they last no longer than wild flowers. Grass withers and flowers fade when the Lord sends the wind blowing over them. People are no more enduring than grass. Grass withers and flowers fade, *but the word of the Lord remains forever.*

Based on Isaiah 40:6-8 (JB)

CONGRATULATIONS

on your completion of <u>Mastering Life with the Twelve Steps of Christian Living</u>.

You have established an important habit over this 70-day period. Reading, praying and reflecting at least twice each day is necessary for personal and spiritual growth.

I urge you to continue in this important process of prayer, reading the Scriptures, and writing.

God's peace be with you.

Ron Keller

PRESENTATION AND WORKSHOP THEMES OFFERED BY THE AUTHOR

1. The Twelve Steps.
   How to use them and experience serenity, fulfillment and intimacy. An introduction to a Christ-centered 12-step lifestyle.
2. Why Americans are doing the Twelve Steps.
   Adolescents, baby boomers, and seniors are discovering freedom, direction and peace through the 12-step process. Why are the Twelve Steps so appealing? (One, two, or three hours.)
3. Youth and the twelve steps.
   How to do the Twelve Steps with youth. A workshop for adults using materials tailored to kids and their needs. Includes complete leader's guide and a fresh, practical strategy for youth ministry. Seminars for senior high youth also available. (Hours or up to two days.)
4. Twelve Step group leader's training.
   Confidence-building for those beginning or developing an existing 12-step group. A seminar integrating prayer, the Scriptures, the Twelve Steps, and basic group processes and skills. (Two days.)
5. Tailored training and retreats.
   These workshop/retreats provide encouragement and affirmation for you and your group. Designed according to your needs. Integration of the Twelve Steps into your context. (Your schedule.)
6. Spiritual direction/career enhancement.
   Personal discipleship and spiritual leadership development. Participants walk through a clearly focused plan for growth and development. (Tailored.)

7. The Twelve Steps for business people. Specific application of the Twelve Steps to those in business struggling to keep healthy priorities and perspective in their lives. (Hours or up to two days.)
8. Know yourself - Know your gifts. An inventory of your strengths and gifts using a broad selection of Scriptural passages and a variety of other aids. Builds confidence and self-esteem. Steps 4, 10 12. (Hours or up to two days.)
9. Your vision for life. Participants develop a thorough vision statement and a workable strategy for personal and professional development. Step 4. (Hours or up to two days.)
10. Developing intimacy. Especially helpful for adult children of dysfunctional families. Experiences in community solitude, and contemplative prayer which lead to greater intimacy with Jesus Christ and others. Step 11. (Hours or up to two days).
11. Discovering freedom and serenity through loss. Through divorce or loss of a loved one, loss of employment, or the end of a relationship, serenity can be experienced. In a deliberate and gentle search we find our own areas of unmanageability and through surrender find fulfillment. Step 1. (Hours or up to two days.)
12. Letting Go. Letting God. In financial crisis, in codependent relationships, struggling for control in uncontrollable situations, or breaking free from unhealthy cultural or family mores we learn to turn our will and our lives over to the care of Jesus Christ as we know him. Steps 2-3. (Hours or up to two days).